MW00464215

Waterlines

Waterlines poems

ALISON PELEGRIN

LOUISIANA STATE UNIVERSITY PRESS ▌▌ BATON ROUGE

Published by Louisiana State University Press
Copyright © 2016 by Alison Pelegrin
All rights reserved
Manufactured in the United States of America
LSU Press Paperback Original
First printing

Designer: *Mandy McDonald Scallan*
Typeface: *Adobe Garamond Pro*
Printer and binder: *LSI*

Library of Congress Cataloging-in-Publication Data
Names: Pelegrin, Alison, author.
Title: Waterlines : poems / Alison Pelegrin.
Description: Baton Rouge : Louisiana State University Press, 2016. | "LSU
    Press Paperback Original."
Identifiers: LCCN 2016012827| ISBN 978-0-8071-6449-5 (paper : alk. paper) | ISBN
    978-0-8071-6450-1 (pdf) | ISBN 978-0-8071-6451-8 (epub) | ISBN 978-0-8071-6452-5 (mobi)
Classification: LCC PS3566.E363 A6 2017 | DDC 811/.54—dc23 LC record available at https://lccn.
loc.gov/2016012827

for Ben and Sam

CONTENTS

ACKNOWLEDGMENTS

Poems from this volume have been published in the following journals: "Background Acting in a Horror Movie with My Son" and "Self-Portrait as a Voodoo Doll" in *Barn Owl Review;* "Keepsakes from the Daily Route" and "Saved" in *Cave Wall;* "Dirty South" in *The Chattahoochee Review;* "The Doomsday Prepper's Villanelle" and "Hot Sauce Shrine" in *The Cincinnati Review;* "My Daguerreotype Boyfriend" in *Crab Orchard Review;* "Funhouse with Chainsaw and Silent Birds," "The Healing Waters of Abita Springs," and "Hurricane Saint" in *The Fourth River;* "Assault F-150" in *Harpur Palate;* "Half-Acre Aubade" and "Saint Tammany Nocturne" in *The New England Review;* "Lines Written after Arson and Three Feet of Rain" in *The Pinch;* "Footnote to My Chronicles of Amazement" and "Full Sturgeon Moon" in *Poetry Congeries;* "The Comet Thief," "The Ghosts of Bayou Fatma," "Paper Charms," and "Parading Around" in *River Styx;* "Crossing the Great Waters" in *Silk Road* (as "Debris"); "Debris" in *Smartish Pace;* "Origami for Marie Laveau" in *Southern Humanities Review;* "Birds of 'Merica," "Heat Lightning in a Strange Land," and "Poem Folded into a Boat and Offered to the Bogue Falaya" in *The Southern Review;* "Swamp Water Baptism" and "The Words You Need" in *Sou'wester;* "Communion with the Rebel Flag," "The Poet Warrior," "Graffiti Jesus" in *The Swamp;* "Ode to New Construction on a Meth Lab Burial Gound" in *Tinderbox;* "Bogue Falaya Death Barge" in *Water Stone Review;* "The Beginner's Side of the Bogue Falaya" and "Dispatch from the Florida Parishes" in *West Branch.*

Special thanks to everyone at LSU Press for making my poetry dreams come true, and to Ava Leavell Haymon for her feedback on earlier versions of this manuscript. To my EfM Group, especially Sherry, Elizabeth, and Rosemary for four years of listening and guidance. My family has always given me time and space to write, and I can never express my gratitude for that gift. To Hubby Bryan Davidson for his unwavering support, and for Ben and Sam, my willing accomplices on many poetry origami adventures.

Waterlines

Poem Folded into a Boat and Offered to the Bogue Falaya

Where will words take me today
and where, silent waters,
will you ship the words
From what troubles shall I be lifted
What will you show me
What do birds speak of in the wet grass
On this journey how many footsteps
how many crickets shall I scatter
If I crouch like this how long
before a fox brushes past
How long since fog lifted its net
and released my soul to leap

Heat Lightning in a Strange Land

Red foxes at dawn are new to us.
We used to have roots—
now we are outsiders drifting

from streets that tell our story,
shipwrecked high and dry
after this last evacuation north

of Lake Pontchartrain, to a new south.
After dark my sons explore
the blacktop, burning their bare feet

and wasting our hurricane batteries
to aim the flashlights everywhere.
I crank the emergency radio

and we serenade fireflies and frogs
because there's hardly cause,
anymore, for its official use.

The mosquito truck passes three times
in a halo of spray. We hold our breath
and run, upending leggy tadpoles

held captive in go-cups.
Heat lightning travels sideways
while we shoot baskets in the driveway.

Nothing can hurt us out here.

Dispatch from the Florida Parishes

I could tell you secrets and lies, but my complaints
are far more interesting. So. In my footprints
are hornets and worms. The garden's wild with aphids,
heather drooping with its fruit of dead bees.
Frogs pour forth plague-style from the fountain's
toxic soup, offering themselves *ad infinitum*
to bare feet, beasts, and wheels, and still
voices remain to herald the afternoon rain.
I struggle with pronunciation and names for things—
waterways, for example, Bogues Chitto and Falaya,
the Tchefuncte, and also nightly arias of coyote aggression.
After said music of yips and yelps, a silver mist
rises to meet the clouds, allowing
the rain less distance to travel and the woodpecker
a flashy entrance, rapid fire jackhammer
to the porch swing and the chimney's flashing,
his mohawk red as the cap of an unlit match.
Things run contrary to the normal order.
In the civilized world nature keeps its distance,
greenery is tamed, held back by fences; here it pulls
with a tangle of countless fingers. Overkill,
but subtle. Trees dragged down, before collapsing,
make storybook tunnels of kudzu interwoven
with pink fizz of mimosa, shading a path one might cross
while passing through the real world to one of myth.
Every morning brings carnage—owl feathers
speared into the grass, June bug wreckage,
ants, their red temples raised overnight, wasp nests
clinging like paper jewels from the branches of cypress.
I choose not to retaliate. My new religion
is solitude, its miracles forever unfolding—
lacewing termite storms, the coolness of a snake
startling the tops of my feet, how the grass whispers
as it sneaks away. I have yet to tire of purple martins
moving like water in the sky, ushering
the sun's retreat on the shores of Lake Pontchartrain.

3

Waterlines

Backfilled marshes passed off as neighborhoods
and segregated by canals, garfish patrolling
the jump rope distance in between—
those are the waters I remember, overflowing
their banks in the slightest rain, leaving rings behind,
tea stains on Saint Francis with a bird in his hand.
I have pedaled a bike through flooded streets,
captained the house from the bay window,
on the lookout for my father wading the last mile
home, his wallet and watch in a garbage bag
above his head. I have crossed the Mississippi
back and again, by ferry and bridge, and once,
in a net of shadows, filled with the urge to jump,
to beat the water at its grayscale game. Below,
the river a concrete smack for those who leap
then sink like rag dolls in silt the dredger clears.
I imagine tripping one life to the next, time slowed
for the long goodbye, all my mysteries answered
just as water smudges the words of this world.

Funhouse with Chainsaw and Silent Birds

Katrina kids living in two worlds—before and after—
my sons look dusty in snapshots meant for the adjustor's
eyes only. Funhouse, post-Katrina snapshots
of pine trees and brick walls all-fall-down.
They must remember evacuating, gridlock exodus,
our homecoming weeks later to soggy phonics bear
lit up, chirping all his words at once.
They must remember me scowling,
chainsaw in hand. I didn't know where to start.
My urge upon returning was to torch the swing set
tangled in uprooted trees, but they were having fun.
They moved me to machete a path to the slide,
to repurpose the contractors' squashed beer cans
as baseballs for them to swat with broomsticks.
Barefoot, delighted, they squealed as droplets
of stale beer or rain water or piss scattered
across the sky, baptizing them. Survivors.
I tried to play along, to make an adventure
of our MRE-surprise food supply, but I suck
at pretending. I started smoking again,
drinking pink wine from a box. I put them to bed
early, while it was still light, just to be done
with something. It was spring before the birds
came back, looking faded, hovering in silence,
not quite sure where to land.

The Beginner's Side of the Bogue Falaya

The river's on the other side of Military Road,
infinite turtles cracked on the trek
to its promise of tire swings and velvet silt.
This side's a patch of swamp that never dries.
Well-water runs clear but tastes of rust,
brews a mud that swallows shoes.
Even puddles wear a skin of oil.

On this side field mice bound
beyond the dog's reach, outside of fence boards
capsized by muscadine vines
that harbor wasps instead of grapes.
No bounty at all.
The garden's yielded one eggplant the size
of a fig and okra in a moat of ants.

No yield but cow bones that surface
like molars through red clay flesh,
birds departing from barbed wire that outlived
its property line to be swallowed by trees.
Walls don't soften the sound of frogs
clinging to the windows, singing down rain.
From inside I count their hearts.

Graffiti Jesus

All Jesus, all the time—it must be
   part of the plan. Jesus in tribal tattoos,
      in burnt toast up for bid on eBay,

in crop circles farmers mow down
   without noticing red-winged clouds
      of common birds lifting from fields of soy.

Scrawny kudzu Jesus, utility pole scarecrow,
   his green cloak offering comfort and shade
      to hitchhikers and their rope-collared dogs.

A mystery man pulsing in the slightest wind,
   not quite the same as the scruffy, muscled youth
      portrayed by the Dove Park Church of God

brow beating from a billboard mid-crucifixion,
   all agony and sweat and warring words—
      Consider your way. I guess nothing is sacred,

that no road trip east to the Gulf Coast casinos
   can ever start off on the right foot. His glare
      troubles me more than what some vandals

backsassed over it in white bubble letters.
   Their profanities burn about as much
      as puffs of smoke. All damnation,

all the time—it can't be true in this world where green
   blunts the edges off of everything, but just in case,
      God forgive my open eyes, my unrepentant gawking.

Background Acting in a Horror Movie with My Son

Nothing Left to Fear (2013)
A family's journey to a better life is interrupted by an unstable man of the cloth.

The director says it's 1993, a carnival somewhere
in Kansas. The priest is evil, and you, my son,
are one of the unborn. Literally. And also in the sense
that you've been told to stare into the camera
with an appetite for flesh. A familiar story—
small-town folk, all petty and fat in the choir, ·
the teenagers up to no good by the river's edge
when a fog rolls in and the water spits up evil.

Sleepy towns are slow to notice demons. The schoolteachers
in their sundresses, even me, your real-life mother,
a background blur fake-tossing baseballs
at a pyramid of cans—we close in as you circle
the fairgrounds with a green balloon tied to your wrist,
never losing the skip in your step. You can't look away
from me and my faux husband, and the roller derby chick
with skulls tattooed on her neck. Our sneers are permanent.

The Doomsday Prepper's Villanelle

The world has gone to shit. On any day
The Good Lord's hellfire caravan will land
And find creation all in disarray.

It will seem like a game we get to play
Until the bullets run dry. I need to plan
For when it hits the fan. Unholy days,

With skies on fire and streets a buckled maze,
Pollute my dreams. Come morning, though, I'm stunned
That sunrise heals the world of disarray.

Apocalypse be damned. I plan to stay
Alive and well and live off of the land.
The world's not shit. I'll reign a thousand days,

By jars of pickled okra—a buffet!—
Made fat. Outside the doublewide I'll stand
And bless creation in its disarray.

Face it—the world is shit, but for today
I'm king with a coonskin cap turned sideways,
my junked yard a scavenger's wonderland,
or a final outpost of disarray.

Saved

Nothing burns me like the touch of believers,
of heavyweights on the healing stage
where they babble nonsense and call it *Holy Spirit.*

A prayer may be said. A hymn may be sung,
hands may be laid, and someone haunted by twitches
is bound to kick over still-warm folding chairs.

A spotlight shined on the ringmaster—
dove gray suit, speckled goatee carved to a point—
as he commanded newcomers to be received,

and that was my sign to get out.
I broke through the cow pasture parking lot
and never looked back at the highway church

with its cover band of high-hats and hallelujahs,
but omens and holy rollers followed me home.
The summer dark turned cold and I swear

a road kill snake sprung at my heel.
The first big rig to sting me with its pebble blast
had *Trust in Jesus* fingered in the dust.

I played it cool through the dark night of my soul,
but there they were next morning, staked out
for the Lord at my back door with pamphlets

and loaves of bread. I've seen this type before,
praying with strangers, subjecting prized tomatoes
to the dark lord of the vegetable patch—

a poisoned crow crucified on a fence post, with black feathers
dropping from the wings pinned back. I've seen them pass
the hat after their horsemen of the apocalypse routine

at the prison rodeo. I've seen cowboy fringe dancing
on their sleeves while they beat down ponies
with braided manes, snuffing the shine

from their eyes so nothing's left but beast.
Then, in white angel boots and burlap wings
they stand in the saddles and fly.

The Ghosts of Bayou Fatma

The view from Google Maps confirms
that what the rich kids teased is true:
where I grew up, all of the houses look alike.
Inside of which did I practice the trumpet?
Where did I prepare my role of gypsy
for dance recital, and earn my porn star
name Comanche Bellemeade, and pray
that Dolly Parton would adopt me
as her daughter? Where is the willow tree
I ran off to, Nashville bound, a fallen angel
in training? Nobody even noticed.

Bystander now, I see the water first.
Tangled snake, a noose around my life,
fringe that swelled and shrank at will.
I never boated on it, or ate from it.
If I fished, it was as a spectator
to the violence of something half-dead
hauled up to the banks, squirming
as I squirmed, while the boys flayed away
with pocket knives and throwing stars,
plotting always for the bigger kill.

All my life I thought it was a canal
across the street in which they rinsed
their hands and the nutria's extracted teeth,
in which I drowned my secrets as offerings
to mammoth catfish down low bottom feeding,
invisible but for whiskers breaching the muck.
I thought it was a canal that ate my diaries,
but on the map I see the name in white,
Bayou Fatma. *Bayou,* another Choctaw word,
and *Fatma,* with a meaning I can't find.

I'll have to die, or pull away from Earth
for the waters to seem blue again.
But for now I am content to zoom,
in warp speed, so that the greens bush out
and then expose the time of day
with cypress tree shadows angled
down the road. I see my driveway
and the dead end sign, water across the street,
houses built on what were wetland woods,
and proof of what I always feared—
catfish, or maybe gar—canoe-sized ghosts
of all the undead things we left behind
thrashing in the mud of Bayou Fatma.

Collect for the Days of My Youth

I remember when I was a child.
I remember my acrobatics,
when I delighted in the world,
touring the neighborhood on a red bicycle.
All things—mud puddle splatters,
goldenrod's secret caves—
all things sang a song of praise.
Take me to those days again,
where afternoons lasted forever
and sunset paused long enough
to bless everything in sight.
It was almost too much,
the world holy and golden,
our laughter incense in the air.

Assault F-150

I never draw on tombstones with pieces of brick.
    I'm careful about who at the beauty shop

sweeps up my hair—because of voodoo, because
    God don't like ugly, and because I'm spooked

even in daylight of the ghosts I might conjure.
    In New Orleans, voodoo would get blamed for deer

splayed open and hung inverted from trees, for an owl's wing,
    its white underside lifting from asphalt to speak

the language of the fan. But in the rural South, across
    Lake Pontchartrain, no one's sneaky about violence.

Blacktop bears the smear of an endless game of assault
    F-150. A pattern—every other mile yields a dead dog

pounded by ritual wheels, the bright entrails spilled
    like a gallon of paint. Shooting skeet and shooting stray wild piglets

that remain after pit bulls pin the boar down for the blade—
    no worries if your aim is off, because all creatures

surrender eventually. All creature fur is rained on,
    swells, until the hind leg lifts and the tanned skin splits—

a feast for articulate crows, and buzzards, mute,
    hunched like tombstones among wasp-haunted fruit.

Owl with No Address

Slump-shouldered totem, ragged owl
looking down with gusto
from crisscrossed power lines,
what ever happened to you?
You took off, I guess, or maybe died,
each breath a tighter fold inward
until your essence dulled,
and disappeared. A perfect end.

But friend, the rains return, the ferns refuel
and re-feather the crooks of trees.
Mushrooms widen their circles.
I press on, walking the dog,
noticing drainage ditch tadpoles flinch.
Scanning fence posts and the fault lines
of lightning-struck pines, when
a wind brushes past, I think of wings.

Red State Epistle

Sunrise, sunset—about the same.
　　Kudzu smothers with the wings

of dirty angels. Everything must go—
　　this summer, its uniform days,

endless rain, frogs
　　that never lose their tails.

Why don't you write?
　　Moths with eye-wings watch

from the coffee shop window.
　　Their time is so short

they're born without mouths.
　　I caught a Jesus fish.

I know I'm dreaming
　　when the boat moves backwards.

The Comet Thief

I used to be the type to wake my children
on blood moon nights, to narrate, next morning,
how we spun through a dome of liquid stars.
Now they read to themselves, and tuck themselves in,
and the night sky is no big deal.
It's too much work to undo *ennui,* to gather them
in the front yard for fireworks that might not show.
I know it's sacrilege to ignore a comet, but
I've got my hands full with soccer mom stuff,
a cloud of Louisiana clay trailing the minivan,
red haze that coats the windshield
and my sunglasses, even the inside of my mouth
like a pinch of sugar or salt. *Wash me please.*
I drag garbage cans to the curb, dodging snails,
and pretend there isn't a comet set to sail tonight,
looking only as high as the fluorescent chorus
of streetlights humming to the beat
of moth bodies batting against the bulbs.
I am the worst of thieves—a corruptor
of amazement—considering I'm still mystified
by my third-grade eclipse, a shadow blessing
that passed its coolness over the schoolyard.
Obedient for once, I locked my eyes
on crescent shadows on the ground,
resisting the flutter in my chest,
the unseen wings tempting my eyes to the sky.

Birds of 'Merica

Anything goes with guns among the bearded ones
of Sportsman's Paradise. If it flies, it dies,
and they field dress it or mount it
on a cypress stump for the man caves
of tomorrow. With swallow-tailed kites
overhead, hawks and kingfishers at rest,
a screech owl whirling from ditch to ditch
across the bike path, I've learned to stifle
my delight for fear they'll be shot,
retrieved by dogs with bites trained
on barbed wire. It's safer to marvel over
plentiful buzzards and crows jaywalking
the entrails buffet, and purple martins
as they bum-rush sunset—too common
or too fast to catch, like flecks of ash
rising into pastel clouds. When birds
drift through my shadow, my pulse stutters
and I think of John James Audubon,
naturalist, disciple of the ways of wings.
Wishing patio-stunned thrushes back to life,
I understand his desire to fan-fold tail feathers
and pin them so, to unpack fluff
from the breast and slice the knotted gizzard
to its stones. But all that work and Audubon's
birds mimic the dead, decoys
nested in the folio pages, where mallards
are minus their jewel tones, and *Great Blue Heron*
stoops unnaturally to fit the page—
stunned, like hunted waterfowl must be
at the instant of sunrise. Duck calls
buzz like kazoos, birdshot soon follows,
then the fall through watercolor skies
towards voices, the grass-tufted marsh,
and boats skirted with palmetto knives and moss.

Self-Portrait as a Voodoo Doll

Chicken livers instead of a heart
and everything hurts.

These button eyes mislead—leaves fallen
to the ground, penny wishes
in the gum-clogged fountain—
they tell me everything is fire.

Spring wastes its pinks on me.

Full moon spooking
through the skylight—
I startle awake with moss in my hair,
afraid to wonder where I've been.

Burlap skin, burlap dress.
I read books upside down,
pick at scabs on my feed-sack flesh
until an arm comes off.

I can't believe what I've become,
muddy feet,
black dogs following everywhere.

Saint Tammany Nocturne

Saint Tammany, I am no contemplative, but I recognize
a blessing taking shape. Lately it has rained so much

that bamboo bends, genuflecting in steam that rises
from the earth. Termites sail the air like sawdust, or snow.

Before the butchery of your name and the sainthood
that followed, you were Chief Tamanend of Delaware Nation.

Peacemaker, the Dutch called you, and also king.
Non-Catholic, non-Christian, but something Assisi-like

in your silence and tribal dress. A stranger to all things bad.
What would you think of your sainthood in the cutthroat

Church of America, of your namesake Parish here,
in Louisiana? As happens with lesser saints, you were forgotten,

shoved aside, banished to the badlands in the west, exiled
south to marshes with muggy, mosquito sunsets. None

of your totem animals followed. Not one of these water birds
is your familiar. In Delaware bronze, you stand on a turtle

with an eagle on your shoulder. Highways crisscross behind,
rush hour choking you with smog, and at night, the burn

of side-swiping snow, the last of red taillights a constant
come-and-go lasso. Among your people, holy man,

a turtle is regal and signifies the earth, but here, turtles
on the highway are flipped over, cracked and festering,

their undersides fish-belly white. Yesterday I spotted one
inching for the centerline from the gravel shoulder.

As though you were watching, I held up traffic
and detoured to Bogue Falaya Park, feeling like a priestess,

or bride, on the pathway laced with catalpa blossoms
and moss. Evening came, rising from misty ditches,

aiming for the sky, but how fitting that the cool air paused,
hovered no higher than my ankles or this turtle's shell.

Communion with the Rebel Flag

I must have backsassed at birth,
so mother soaped the drawl
from my mouth, along with *dis* and *dat*
and the taste of slurs, the songs
of my people and their laments,
leaving me orphaned, a mute
in the vaudeville act. She threatened
suds at the first syllable of slang,
but her plan backfired, and sometimes
that drawl escapes. Angry or drunk
is when I sound like what I am,
a coonass mystic, courteous but resentful,
defeated daughter of a last-place state,
tormented by my family name recorded
in the Confederate book of the dead.
A rebel, but I'm not sure against what.
I'm proudly AWOL from the worst
of southern culture's hostilities.
I've told redneck jokes and sipped
from the *I have a dream* coffee mug on which,
hot beverage added, red states fade to blue,
but like a lapsed Catholic I can stand up,
sit down, and say the words. I confess
not solidarity but a soft spot for chutzpah
in the underdog since reading
that Confederate statues face north
out of defiance, and I have milked the drawl
to get what I want out of strangers.
And is this not southern pride? Am I not
proud—ambassador between worlds,
mingling undercover on pontoon boats
among sportsmen with trapper beards.
I'm offended, but I drink their beer
and live in limbo between worlds,
both everything and nothing
I was taught to be.

Paper Charms

It is bad luck to fall down on Mondays,
and you never step over a baby any day of the week
or look at your sweetheart through the window.
Paper charms work written in blood
or mud puddle ink. If you hate somebody,
write down your grudge and bury it in bamboo
where the bad luck birds come to roost.
You shouldn't ask what howls
because I'll have to tell you it's the loup-garou.
Don't mock an owl. Dreams of horses
are good, but a dream of pigs means death.
To rid yourself of a neighbor, kill a rooster
and throw it over his house on a night
when it rains and the moon glows red.
Touch a corpse to keep your magic
fresh, but beware of blood stains—once
you kill, no sleepwalker will ever lead you to gold.
For healing, midwifery, and aches and pains,
rub a live mole to death between your hands,
but don't let it bite you. To hurry love,
gut a hummingbird and smear the nectar
of its insides over what you want. Cover your tracks,
sweep up your debris, but never after dark.
An eyelash is enough to give a rag doll life.
You can't give black magic back. One trip
to the crossroads and the red clay seam inside your arm
will never wash away. Your prayers turn black
and haints become bold toward you in the mist,
holy shadows held hostage until, with a hook
poked through a fish's eye, you prick a talisman tattoo.

Lines Written after Arson and Three Feet of Rain on a River Named "Rest among the Pines"

(Three Versions)

I.

The Indians who named it Tickfaw,
would they fish the river
now that it's been spoiled by pontoon boats,
a hot spot for wet t-shirts
and houseboat squatters tethered
on the tupelo side, mostly abandoned
these three days in fear of a named storm?
Clouds trump the time of day
and I'm in bed early with a flashlight
and a swig from every bottle,
dredging dreams of an earlier flood.
I was six, and it was near dark
before dad got home, soaked
to the chest, his company car
abandoned on the neutral ground.
This time I don't know why I stayed put
with the you-loot-we-shooters. Maybe
just to see, to be one of the ones
in the hardware store who can show
with hands spread wide how tall
the water stood, to have grilled
a season of meat gone soft
in the deepfreeze, testifying
at the post office and the Piggly Wiggly
to three straight days of rain
and the out-of-nowhere arson fires.

II.

When I have trouble dozing off
I count the times Miss Hawaiian Tropic

Middle Age has poured me the poison
I live by. Then I court the short sleep

with solitaire and Dewar's over ice,
buzzing deep into a repeat dream

of nothing but arson fire for the moon
to see by, the Frog's Breath charred

to the pilings, payback personified.
What's left for us, what will we do

without a watering hole and a place
to gas the boats and buy live bait?

Boredom turns south fast—darts
at the corkboard, the doorframe, the ceiling.

You light matches when you're bored,
and what harm is fire in the worst rain

you'll ever know? Almost
witchcraft, the way people trickled

out of hiding when they heard kids
belly-flopping from the landing—

into the water a thousand times
where the Frog's Breath used to stand,

thinking, *what luck,*
school closed and now this.

III.

Nothing but haze. Hip boots are not high enough
when the holdouts emerge in smaller boats
to take inventory, as if summoned
for a headcount at the end of days.
The Frog's Breath is gone, and some say
the waterline, clumps of moss caught
along the tips of chain link fences, was never near
this high. One thing is sure—the river
needs a louder name when it swells past the dock,
steering palmettos like schools of fish,
dragging trash from the burn piles,
then heavier things, a magnet nothing can resist.
Everything looks the same. Three days of tequila
and speed, and there is no talking sense to Jimmy—
he fights the war on two fronts, firing shots
at looters and lookers, both. The rest of us
set to grill the best cuts first, fillet and flank.
The moon aflame keeps us up dealing,
all night cutting the deck, rotating seats
in the otherwise-good-for-nothing Airstream
with the only air conditioner for miles,
passing stories, rumors, concern around
like matches from some vacation restaurant
with a name nobody would believe.

Crossing the Great Waters

I've seen debris, water closing over streets, floating balls
of ants, manhole covers that levitate and leak fish—
and yet a flood was something I looked forward to.
Fondue dinner at dusk, saints I could believe in
keeping watch from hurricane candles
while we slept. Half the year, beginning June first,
we prepped for "the big one"—photo albums
on a top shelf, the pantry stocked with canned stew.
Card games for those days of water, water lapping past
the threshold, soaked up by walls that darkened
like a granite slab in rain. Water always wins.
I'm nearly dead of hurricanes. I have traveled by pirogue
the grid of city streets erased by flood—not
as the crow flies, but as a snake might ribbon
through sludge in a ditch. Poled to the hospital,
asthmatic, barely breathing, my mother banging
a paddle on the glass door clamped shut, the doctors
banging back. I fought off sleep when what I wanted
was to float away, buoyed in a roux of mud,
the canal's backwash, swamp broth from which
birds somehow emerge immaculate.

Keepsakes from the Daily Route

Cigarettes and Swisher Sweets rise from the ditches
    as they fill with rain, and this, and asphalt steam,
feels exotic in a way. I do not travel often or well,

    like my uncle who shrimped off his boat with a girly name,
green wing nets dragging like a witch's hair. He knew
    the water's drag, moody in each of its seasons,

walked steady on his boat, but on pavement
    stumbled like a drunk, wild with stories of a past life
offshore for two week stretches, welding

    in tight spaces, in his downtime fishing off the rig
for sharks. It must count for something,
    knowing by a bird's flight the water's mood.

There are no keepsakes from his daily routes
    through bayous, Lakes Maurepas and Pontchartrain,
and sometimes out to the Gulf. Never a shark's tooth

    or puffer fish in high alarm, personified, shellacked,
with googly eyes and a tiny straw hat. No snow globe
    with mosquitoes swirling in puddle water before settling,

slow as ash, on a riverboat, a pelican's shoulders,
    or Saint Louis Cathedral. Why shouldn't souvenir waters stain,
bring us to our knees, churn about the pine tree spires in the sky?

My Daguerreotype Boyfriend

"where early photography meets extreme hotness"

You, with a prophet's name, posed
on a zebra rug in side-buttoned boots,
sneak past the shushing librarian

and find me, damsel jailed in a tower
of books. We'll never touch,
though I'm a sucker for footballers,

for crew teams lined up by height,
for poets and priests, and horse thieves
sentenced to hang, explorers chopping

through Arctic seas never to return.
No need to sleep *en plein air*
on haystacks—peace-tie your cutlass

and come to mama. There is room
in my life for the outlaw who smokes
on camera in cuff links and a paper collar,

the Thoreau look-alike, the frontiersman
dressed in skins, his beard carved
by a Bowie knife. I favor equally

the cowboy with the shot-off finger
and the Indian with an eagle feather
stuck in his hatband. I'm so alone,

the archives' nun, reading in the dark,
feeling around the metal shelves
for something warm. I don't care

what people say. I have resigned myself
to an old fashioned courtship
of rationed touch. Certainly you

recognize my silhouette,
the blushing scent I drag along
in these heavy skirts, my costume

for the hunt. I coo like a dove in flight,
and you always listen—lifting your chin
first and then your eyes, squinting

as though from the crow's nest,
over desert seas, you've sighted
promised land.

Dirty South

Am I untrue? Does it spit in the face of jazz
and my treasured drawl if secretly I envy
more civilized places, with fewer drag races
and racists? Elsewhere. Away
from the chemical burn of refinery fires,
out of reach of hurricanes. I want to shed
this fear I have of snapping any second,
of falling in step with my rebel yell uncles
and their trigger-happy tirades. But I've oversimplified,
maybe even lied about their good hearts, kind
upfront, and in a way, colorblind. If there were
a tent, revival white, nearby, maybe I'd parade
the aisle in a sweat, let the true believers
lay hands and tug the traitor out of me, rekindle
raging loyalty instead. Perhaps it's time
to accept my fate, renew my vows to the dirty south
on nighttime's altar, its engine of insect noise.
Hating them would be easiest, but after all this time
I find my eyes adjusting to the light.

Swamp Water Baptism

Hold me under long enough and I'll speak in tongues,
apologize for anything. Bring it on, and bring me to my knees,
give me levees anchored in shifting clay, and when
the levees break blame it on me for being a product
of the dumping-ground south, one fool among many who believe
that we can pray the flood away by kneeling on rice, rubbing
rosaries and garden statues, their faces carved with blank stares.
And when a backwash tide swallows the streets,
unmoor the shotgun houses, float them like barges cut loose,
with toddlers and their grandmothers in wheelchairs
backsliding down rooftops, vanishing in slow-sinking swirls.
Say, "I told you so," to signs of surrender—white flags
of house dresses poked through attic shutters
on the eraser ends of walking sticks, muffled
lamentations. Swamp water baptism—hold me under long enough
and I'll apologize for anything. Cajun boat brigade
navigating the streets in a stolen fleet—I'll tell them to pass me by.
I say Uncle. I give up. If it floods again I'm never coming back.

Footnote to My Chronicles of Amazement

Amazement, my first rebellious act,
ahead of beer or boys. I would sneak out
to the canal, streetlights
but no houses yet on the other side.
Knowing the danger of snakes,
I tiptoed beneath the scorn of owls
and through the willow tree's
beaded curtain, walked a plank
of corrugated pipe to marvel
at alligator gar gliding single file
through sludge. Untouchable,
untroubled by my brother's arrows
and thrown rocks, they seemed
stepping stones to another world.
I never crossed their bridge.
I renounced such primitive joys
and instead spent summers
twirling a baton. Baptized
by smoke bombs and bonfire ash,
my heart grew a shell which remained,
until recently, uncracked,
much to my amazement.

Debris

I drive the Gulf Coast to get away,
but this Mississippi debris seems familiar.
What's left is front steps leading nowhere,
the waterline, oak trees trimmed with car parts.

This Mississippi debris seems familiar.
Plywood everywhere. I need some time off
from waterlines and oak trees trimmed with car parts.
Debris shingles my memory lane.

Plywood everywhere. I need time off.
There's a yellowed snapshot of me here.
Debris shingles my memory lane,
no landmarks left. Where am I again?

There's a snapshot of me here, or close to here,
with a sea lion planting kisses on my cheek.
No landmarks left. Where am I again?
What happened to the Oceanarium?

Once, a sea lion kissed me on the cheek.
Dolphins rode out the storm in swimming pools.
What happened to the Oceanarium?
The storm surge clawed it out to sea?

Dolphins rode out the storm in swimming pools.
The gift shop, where dad bought me a jewelry box,
the storm surge clawed it out to sea.
On Sundays we used to picnic here.

Dad bought me a cedar jewelry box.
The air smells sweetly of hurricane debris.
On Sundays we used to picnic here,
landscape of front steps leading nowhere.

Angel of Loss

August 30, 2014
(nine years and one day post-Katrina)

The angel of loss felled trees
upon my house, dragged me through fire
and debris armored with rusting nails,
and rinsed my wounds and wiped my tears
with the reach of filthy gray-scale waves.
And I thought I was dead because my heart
lost its wings and petrified, a brick
inside my chest, and I couldn't fight it.

I was jailed, or I was dead, and the walls
were debris that grew all night.
It was always night,
and I was so emptied of soul
I could not lift a hand to clear the dirt
from my face. The rain never answered
when I wondered why.

By miracle or curse I came home,
but at first there were no doors, no walls, no beds,
only echoes and a stench resurrected
with footsteps and coughs.
Inside, outside, I found
one cardinal, then another and another
drowned in a net of fallen branches,
and the kitchen drawers all held water.
I hammered all my fingers numb,
and I was haunted in dreams by the drowned,
and by bloated books, and all those words lost to the sky.

Nine years, and time has watered down my rage
like rain that makes a muddy ditch run clear.
Out of control, I pulled out my hair
and drank too much. Everyone did.
I knifed the air mattress when I was done with it,
and there is a song in there, somewhere,
all blues notes. My sons were afraid of me,
but I'm no longer nearly dead of hurricane.
The anniversary sneaks past.

I still have dust in my cough
and I don't sleep much, keeping vigil instead
with nighttime's angel, moon that fades
so slowly I mistake the gray light for daybreak,
and stirring birds for giant drops of rain.
Grief is done with me for now.

For so long I was mute, empty of praise, but now
I lose my footing when I step into a spray
of daylight. I do not know the word
for such a stumbling,
but until I do I'll call it *awe*.

The Words You Need

May you find the words you need. May you mutter in sleep,
and may the talk run over into morning's pale skirts
and steamed mirrors. May a madness possess your mouth,
and may one day the curses lift, a sudden anthem
of clouds revoked from the hypnotic, blinding sun.
May you see cursive when you stargaze.
Words in the sand and words in the sound of the surf.
When you open your mouth, let hornets swarm. In other words,
may your insults sting. May you wake one day
fluent in birdsong and the Arabic of scattered seed.
Midwestern words aplenty should you desire
to praise blackbirds pitching on tassels of corn,
and a southern drawl when you need to bewitch.
May God whisper in your ear God's name,
the syllables shifting like an opal's hues.
May you object with graffiti on the sides of trains.
May you welcome the blues, words tattooed on your chest,
unerasable psalms running the length of your scars.
Curse like your shirt's on fire and let every breath be a prayer.
May you witness cherry blossoms surrender,
and, in surrendering, utter an opera of sighs
as the wind shudders through the leaves.
May you be wise in the way of mystics
who know that sometimes words are not enough
and who then welcome silence in the shadows of flowering trees.

Hot Sauce Shrine

I used to be a high priestess of tail-feather feel-good
mumbo jumbo, naysayer extraordinaire
cobbling together some crazy quilt catechism
to cling to as I tangled in the world's thorns,
frantic, fearing the chill soon to come.
I haven't turned holy roller or handler of snakes,
but things changed slowly, or all at once.
Maybe it was when I drove through a dust devil
and inhaled its grit of cut grass and cigarette butts.
I've taken to praying since the whirlwind
shook me loose, or anyway I dip my head
at stoplights until I get distracted by scenery,
or birds, and the prayers come out confused.
I'm clueless—my angel of place smokes blunts
and speaks to me in bug bite braille. I know
to visit Saint Roch and turn his statue to the wall,
but I hunger for alone time on an island
with an organ that plays itself, or to whisper
all my secrets to the hot sauce shrine.
I read that the world is a dream of God,
and now I don't know what to do with my hands.
The world is God's dream and I am a sparrow
passing through song and the brass glow of fire,
or maybe that is wrong, and I'm trapped inside,
stunned against the glass or down the chimney,
terrified of kind hands that sweep me to the door.
When I wake I'm walking the moonlit labyrinth
with wet feet, and the birds are quiet because
I have terrified them with the thunder
of my stumbling. Oh God of everything that creeps,
I light a candle and ask my question:
Is it pilgrimage enough if I spend my life
remembering the few seconds I was a bird?

Parading Around

It just so happens I am sick of parades.
I am tired of barbequing behind barricades, all day
wading in a stream of peanut shells and garbage,
the key to a Porta Potty on a shoelace around my neck.

I am ashamed of the change that comes over me,
friendliest member of a crowd. I become grabby,
a hand stomper, mother of sons trained to leap before tractors
for a thrown spear, foam football, or trinkets that shine.

People waving, bells when I walk—I am a parade of one.
The spindly goat man that creeps behind, silhouette
with horns or a beaked nose, bulbous papier-mâché skull
like a light bulb gone out—he's my costumed shadow.

I'm hung over. I hate the smell inside of masks, hair dye
that doesn't fade, stray, fluorescent feathers on my tongue
weeks later, long after the Mardi Gras Indians
have hushed their drums and packed their headdresses away.

I have tried to remain uncostumed and far away—
in the suburbs, or on side streets, in the shadows of retirement homes.
But even there, the elders are busy festooning wheelchair wheels
and walking sticks with braided crepe paper and sequins.

Dog parades. Boat parades. Kings and courts. Stepping clubs
swapping kisses for tissue-paper flowers. Buck-toothed beauty queens
riding in convertibles, clowns in dune buggies. Flambeaux. Diesel fumes.
Having worn out my shoes, I limp as I follow the funky brass.

I wave my pocket square as a sign of surrender. Give me Taps.
A horse with no rider. A twenty-one gun salute. I fantasize
about the solemnity of funerals where people actually weep
and then ride away down rain-slicked streets in limousines.

Give me a smudge of ash on my forehead.
Give me fasting and fish on Fridays.
This year I offer up the roller derby running of the bulls,
I'll skip the skates, horns, the tutu, and wiffle bats.

This year, come Twelfth Night, I'm leaving town for someplace
where it snows snow rather than Silly String. I'm learning to ignore sirens,
to resist looking back at the parade that follows me everywhere,
the comet sparkling down streets filthy with satire and flashing lights.

Poem Folded into a Crane and Left in the Hands of Saint Francis

Ever-silent chapel, I have made
my own answer of you to me,

cribbed a religion of shadow
and mote and prayer book open

to the perfect psalm. I can barely make out
what the natural world reveals

through imperfect glass.
When in doubt I add wings to it.

Pause of clarity at vespers—
wind-spun kaleidoscope outside,

birds springing branch to branch
like thumbprints of ash.

I forgot my question to the dragonfly
but I've received an answer—

yes to everything, yes, yes.

Full Sturgeon Moon

Guitar hero neighbor, how does he live?
I wonder if he looked outside last night
and noticed me hot-footing on asphalt,
in pajamas, hunting down a better view
of the green corn moon, myriad names
for its beauty, each facet of which for me
was obscured by clouds. August moon may have escaped,
but with neighbor I have the upper hand,
having toured his house while it was being built,
and kicked up echoes in the bonus room
where now he practices guitar. It occurs to me
that I am the opposite of a traveling poet.
Some nights I fall asleep watching TV—
can he see me through the transom windows?
Standing in the driveway safe from snakes,
I am missing out on noteworthy things
such as tiny skulls minus half their teeth.
It is someone's job to spray poison
in ditches where mosquitoes breed,
and someone else's to mow down sloppily
elephant ears and hyacinth that offer shelter.
Neighbor, guitar hero, and builder of guns,
I am not the only one who listens, but also geckos
with peppered backs rippling down the front door's
leaded glass. Meanwhile, what might also be named
lotus moon illuminates us all.

Thunder Psalm

Lord God of thunder, of wave,
of shadows haunting every surface
on the earth your jewel,
why the doubt in my bones?
Why does my soul growl?
This world, once paved with turquoise pools,
is now a sponge for blood,
is shrouded in dust
from the droughted fields.
I know you have hidden yourself,
but where? Like a fool I trample
labyrinths and gardens,
I walk until I lose my footing
in the terror-filled sea.
I write my name in dust,
or erase my name from the dust,
I couldn't say which.

The Poet Warrior

Rural carrier, deliverer of bad news, yesterday
you brought a royalties statement and—low blow!—
documentation of a year in which so few copies moved
there was no point in them cutting a check.
And so it is with both seriousness and a wink
that I am moving on, revoking my book of devotions
to the Dirty South and offering it instead as a gift
to the people of South America, to nuns that pinch,
and to falconers starving down their birds in the dark.
Publisher, I beg you not to pulp! These poems
have traveled shotgun, my front seat comrades,
companions through carpool and the car wash.
If you have given up on my book, recycle the pages
into paper dolls, hole punch confetti, usher wishes
into being with a thousand thousand origami cranes.
In my dreams, and in my poems, I can fly.
I cross my backyard swamp by moonlight,
for backup a rescue dog with webbed feet whose
barking at all that moves has rid my yard of birds.
Someone (me!) stood here (the woods behind my house!)
watching clouds race across the moony dark
and reached the conclusion that locusts revving at dusk
is as good a sound as any to die to, if die we must.
Are there locusts in South America? Are there spiders
that anchor monstrous webs of gold to stop signs
and power lines? I ask these questions of no one,
moving my lips like a village mystic, the last speaker
of her language spitting out curses, or prayers.

Origami for Marie Laveau

Saint Peter holds the key to everything
and for this the devoted kissed his toes away.

You've also been eroded, dame of rumors
and blood that won't scrub clean. Pilgrims

on haunted tours of Saint Louis Cemetery #1
crowd your grave, recently vandalized pink,

pinching off chips of brick or filling vials
with cemetery dust. What are their petitions?

What's this idiot's altar, crime scene
of trinkets, filthy ropes of fishnet lace,

and graffiti wishes etched in red brick chalk?
Vulgar, spangled, superstitious debris—

I've lit candles, and walked the labyrinth, left
crumpled bills on an altar of braided loaves,

held tight the lucky fava bean, but only
as a backup plan. Usually I toss my paper birds

to fountains or the chapel garden where I hope
my ashes might take root. These few today,

like all your favors, will sweat their colors
through rain and heat, or find themselves

archived in the pockets of thieves. Fools
lean in close and wince at the whir of bats

and darker things. They say no spirit remains
once the soul exits and the eyes are thumbed shut,

but something follows. My ankles itch
with the touch of invisible ferns.

Hurricane Saint

In summer, when the rain breaks and the hallowed scrim
of dusk appears, my palms twitch, I ache for votives
slick with icons and sweat, for the gift of signs
to tease omens out of sputtering wicks.

It's written in me, to see clearly when the waters rise,
to walk the grocer's aisles stirring up dust, worrying buttons
and beads. I've known Disaster Aid food stamps.
I have bought pork chops and felt ashamed,

yet a storm charted elsewhere grieves me more
than it relieves me, my flashbacks a sad substitute
for sucking wet air, or standing at the sink for a cat bath
with a stack of pre-moistened towelettes.

The Gulf Coast martyrs itself against storm wheels.
Supplicant grasses bow down, trees tear themselves apart.
I keep vigil from home. There are hordes of us, holdouts,
wandering halls like ghosts, or nuns in a darkened cloister,

the windows fitted with plywood. I always wanted
to be the afflicted one, the girl in the choir
who speaks in tongues, and now it falls to me to honor
the violent waters and wind that christened me.

Bogue Falaya Psalm

Do you hear my song
when I stand on the bridge
Were these waters ever clear
Where do you hide in this world of silt
Inside of which cypress tree
pinned against winter
I know your silence
as tides in my mind
polishing dull words
into prayer
After every downpour
I am afraid I'll drown
The river rewrites its banks
Some days my net is empty
but there are fish enough
to feed us all

The Healing Waters of Abita Springs

"Where nature performs miracles."

Healing powers? In these egg-tasting waters?
We use them to make beer, to refill plastic milk jugs
with trickles from a bearded spigot. I don't need

the trailhead sign or a sexy, bronze squaw statue
to remember that in the sugar pot my goldfish dwell
in the tears of an Indian princess, that Main Street

was a Choctaw village first, snuffed out
by New Orleanians who traveled here to "take
the waters" and outwit yellow fever. Delirium's

a full-time resident now, plaguing us with dust devils
and motorcycle deaths on Hwy 36, asphalt mirages
traversed by a caravan of half-starved dogs.

I mistrust the surface waters, their mud mixing
with elixir bubbling from beneath—too much like an oil spill
and its waterline of ooze smudging every boat

that passes. They say creek-side, in the flesh of spotted gars,
Choctaw ghosts wait for drunks to unzip, slip,
then thrash themselves tight in honeyed silt. As for the missing,

can't call them drifters now, this crew that slumbers
on picnic tables, beneath the trestle bridge bewitching
river bass onto hairpin hooks—it's wild berry artesian

moonshine that holds them close, like bees in amber.
They mutter devotions with their dusty mouths
to a patron saint that drops down wallets thick with bills.

And summer nights, just like the living, they dance, they fade
into the Opry crowd, the wind behind them swirling
leaves in hoodoo circles that never quite settle down.

Ode to New Construction on a Meth Lab Burial Ground

Not often have I tasted ceremony, but I remember
taking orders from an Indian named Snowbear,
who, as darkness flooded our 8th grade campout,
tied us to trees with thread he dared us not to snap,
and I won the bet, motionless while millipedes
poked me like fingers from the grave, silent
when he called *game over,* a wild thing openly hiding,
silent and brave and still even as his boots
trampled through fallen leaves with steps
that sounded like brush fire; Outward Bound,
but I thought I was a Native child, and I have tried
to return to that day when I lingered between worlds,
but instead I am a gawker in the Florida Parishes,
where it's never quite safe—sunset, for example,
through the pine trees' bristles, is just
a fire with teeth, and there is fire everywhere—
burn piles, brush fires, smoke pits stuffed with boar,
lazy fires set in paint cans on purpose and left
unsupervised for the firefighters to find, only
they themselves are—how shall I say it—lackadaisical—
lite on water, heavy on wait-and-see, meanwhile
the woods consume themselves, while down the road
the meth lab rages, that took the boy and his father
who entered the inferno after him, and almost certainly
too late, the softbellies of Fire District #12 rolled in;
short on hydrants and sleep, they hauled water
in tanks that Houdini in his straitjacket
would have aimed for, and it was magic they needed,
or a miracle, but only morning answered, along with smoke
speaking its language of the snake, yet within six months
the dump trucks delivered mounds of red clay,
and, like that, the earth was on fire again, which is how
the Choctaw and Tchefuncte pre-fabbed Louisiana,
by hauling woven baskets of earth to add a shoulder

or a wrinkle or spoked wheel, making sacred spaces
for us to desecrate, because we forget who came before,
and we always hate the ones who come after us,
for the change they bring, their unfamiliar dust,
their army of surveyors applying machetes
to the tender undergrowth, claiming another rancid slab
of swamp for a housewife with paint chip dreams;
does she know about the fire, the teddy bear shrine,
that the boy continues, stalled at three years old,
how I can almost see him in footy pajamas, pouting,
dragging his sooty blanket down the garden path
of the new house where new children scream and kick
at the sky on their swing set, fresh-stained cedar
anchored in a mound where the meth lab used to be,
where he lay mute until his dreams smoked out,
beside his father who went back in after him—
each drive-by it's a different nightmare, but always
the trees lean in, their lesser branches charred.

Half-Acre Aubade

I agree that the possum is worthy of praise, so I sing
with my dog as the darkness shifts to pink,
mash my face against the glass door and marvel

as the grizzled marsupial plunders the cat bowl on the porch.
Such a struggle to stifle the growl festering in my throat,
the urge to run through wet grass without the tight collar of clothes.

Yes, I am like this shelter dog, and also the neighbor's donkey,
longing to cloak myself in the musk of the earth by rolling
in manure and the rained-on, deflated shapes of dead animals.

The humidity-warped compass of the fan blades twirls
north, south, east, and west all at once. Today has arrived!
The neighbors celebrate by riding a golf cart

down the gravel drive to collect the newspaper, and I walk
the asphalt, coffee cup in one hand, axe helve in the other
to defend against snakes or the bricklayer's pit bulls

with ears shaved close to their heads. The sun ignites
the bell of the water tower and the unsteady fire tower, shines
on the sex offenders sheltered on United Church Road

outed by postcards listing their tattoos and rapes.
This morning, this routine morning, is unlike any other.
I open the garage only to see a crawfish war-painted in mud

strutting up the drive, pincers raised in two-pronged applause,
a boiling pot Atlas losing his balance, calling on me
to shoulder the world, to praise what there is to praise.

Bogue Falaya Death Barge

Maxime, self-stranded pillar saint,
will save the angels time by climbing
to glory in a chapel of clouds,
and in Tibet, to transcend the flesh,
monks fast for years on seeds
and weak tea, reduced to the lotus pose
and a once daily pealing of a bell.
After years of silence the tomb is unsealed,
and if the flesh appears mummified
their lips are painted gold,
and they are worshipped as gods.
Even Louisiana has a homegrown intercessor,
Catherine, the little Cajun Saint,
who died sweetly of leukemia,
leaving behind a cult of devoted
bathed by her oily tears.

Desert tombs and sainthood
aren't for me. I'm scrappy,
mouthy, and lazy when it comes
to sacrifice. I fall too often away
from wonderment and predict I will fight,
even against a death of ease.
But one ritual I could embrace
would be the death poem—
articulation of the final lucidity,
a prayer to paper, origami square
fit for an angular sparrow, or fox.

In another life, in Japan, I could write
that I have begun the descent down Mount Fuji,
only to find that snow is the same on both sides.
Here, I'm bound to heat and words of water,
because even as the world loosens its hold
on me, the rivers are slow to release.
What else is worth saying?

The days wind down, I drag my hand
through the moon's golden scribble
on the river.
   I'm amazed yet again by frog song
and snowfall stars, but there's no more changing
the words inked on my paper boat.

NOTES

The Bogue Falaya River flows through Washington and Saint Tammany Parish, past Covington, Louisiana, and into the Abita River. Its name comes from two Choctaw words: *bogu,* meaning "river," and *falaya,* meaning "long."

"Background Acting in a Horror Movie with My Son": *Nothing Left to Fear* (2013), starring Anne Heche and Justin Brown.

"Assault F-150:" Visitors to voodoo priestess Marie Laveau's tomb in Saint Louis Cemetery #1 sometimes mark 3 Xs on her tomb with red brick in order that she might grant them a wish.

"Saint Tammany Nocturne": Chief Tamanend was a peace-loving member of the Delaware Nation of Pennsylvania. He had many affectionate nicknames, among them Patron Saint of America, and though he never traveled south, he is the namesake of Saint Tammany Parish in Louisiana.

"Paper Charms": I learned about some of these superstitions by reading two old books my father studied when he gave bus tours of New Orleans and of plantation homes: Lyle Saxon's *Old Louisiana,* and *Gumbo Ya-Ya: A Collection of Louisiana Folk Tales,* compiled by Saxon, Robert Tallant, and Edward Dreyer. The loup-garou is the Cajun version of the werewolf.

"Lines Written after Arson and Three Feet of Rain on a River Named 'Rest among the Pines'": Tropical storm Allison, June 2001

"My Daguerreotype Boyfriend": http://mydaguerreotypeboyfriend.tumblr.com/

"The Words You Need": The poet Camille Dungy inscribed the phrase "May you find the words you need" into my copy of her poetry collection *Smith Blue* when she signed it for me at the 2102 AWP book fair in Chicago.

"Origami for Marie Laveau": Vandals covered her tomb in pink latex paint in 2013, and since its restoration the Archdiocese of New Orleans has restricted access to all of Saint Louis Cemetery #1.

"Bogue Falaya Death Barge": I learned of Maxime the Pillar Saint from a photo essay by Amos Chapple.